Tina,

God Bless. Enjoy!

Kristina Gise

4 Ways to Make a Change

4 Ways to Make a Change

Kristina Gipe

Copyright © 2021 Kristina Gipe
All Rights Reserved.
ISBN 978-1-7373436-0-8

Dedication

Enrico Fabrizi, thank you for your assistance with this writing project and helping me gather ideas about the fear of the unknown. Thank you for listening and your assistance with the project ideas and the layout of the information. Keep sharing your ideas and leadership journey with others, you continue to make an impact on many lives.

This book is dedicated to all those who never stop reaching and keep pursuing their goals and dreams. Keep moving forward as you seek to grow and change one step at a time.

Contents

CHAPTER 1 Seeking a change? 1

CHAPTER 2 Identify the want or need. Ask yourself, "What?" 5

CHAPTER 3 Why, Why, Why…... 19

CHAPTER 4 How am I going to get there?.. 35

CHAPTER 5 The When... 49

CHAPTER 6 You can!... 61

CHAPTER 1

Seeking a change?

Y ou most likely picked up this book because you have some reason you want to make a change in your life. We all do. Sometimes it is just a matter of starting and sticking with it, or other times it is a matter of where to even begin. The thing or things we want to change often vary depending on our day, our emotions, or a variety of other reasons. We all want more for ourselves, I believe it's a natural feeling. Perhaps that's why at times in our lives we may come across as hard to please, stubborn, set in our ways - you name it!

Do you feel you're spinning your wheels trying to make a change in your life, or that you should be farther ahead than you are? There is no worse feeling than that of spinning your wheels and getting nowhere. Better yet, how many times have you given up on that change you are trying to make?

4 Ways to Make a Change

If we're honest with ourselves, probably more times than we can count on one hand. I know I have. It isn't easy to make transitions in our life and sometimes it is a matter of giving ourselves a chance. There is very likely a strong reason behind this change you are seeking to make in your life. We don't wake up one day with a to-do list simply to make one. We make a to-do list because there are things we want or need to get done.

We all have changes we want to make at different times in our lives. If we didn't want to change something at some point in our lives, they wouldn't be exciting. Also, sometimes change comes our way as a result of something we didn't plan for and we have to make adjustments because of it. Other times change is exciting, and we want to experience a new feeling in life. Whatever the reason, I want you to remember throughout reading this book that you can make a change.

> This is most likely a reason you have created a list for your life, because you want to accomplish more for your life. That to-do list we create gives us a feeling of something to work on or towards. It can provide us structure for our day.

This is most likely a reason you have created a list for your life, because you want to accomplish more for your life. That to-do list we create gives us a feeling of something to work on or towards. It can provide us structure for our day. The same can be said of our lives: creating change takes structure and provides stability in our lives as we feel better about who we are on the way to where we want to be.

Each checkmark on your daily to-do list provides a feeling of achievement in your day. The same can be found in creating goals in your

Seeking a change?

life. Make your to-do list excite you, not deflate you. Afterall, this is your life, your change and ultimately your challenge. Your victory will be through you only. No one else will be able to set your passion, your drive, your reality.

As much as we try to cross things off of our checklist, that list can also be one of a constant reminder of all we have done. It can be our steps on our journey to who we want to become. Think about it, reflect upon it, and grow because of it! Those checkmarks are like footprints in the sand. Each one holds meaning. Each one has purpose.

Who or what is stopping you? The answer to this question is most likely to be ourselves. Why we delay things only we can answer. However, change lies within the grasp of each one of us. Whether on a small or larger, more complex scale, the way to starting any change begins with us and our willingness to try and take that first step.

Identify your goals, talents, and unique abilities through setting the steps. You have many things to offer. In identifying the reason we want to change, through the what, why, how, and when, we can gain more out of life. This will take a lot of reflecting and the willingness to dig deep within ourselves beyond the surface of the true reason we want to change.

Imagine a life that has changed as a result of doing more for yourself. I am not saying be selfish, but simply really digging deeper into your feelings and emotions to become who you want to be. This is possible, and what better time for it than now? Choose today to take those simple steps and create a new journey with much progress and celebration. Get ready to celebrate who you are. To feel proud of yourself, feel more accomplished and celebrate the changes you strive to make in your life each day.

Every day we are given many hours. What we do with that time is up to us, but in the end we can do more for ourselves if we choose. Life keeps moving forward, and how we move along with it is also up to us, but we should always strive to move and not simply get carried through life. There are relationships to be built, ideas to be shared, and endless opportunities and possibilities for us to paint a beautiful canvas. Grab hold of today and make the best of it. Today holds much value: explore the possibilities that lie within it for you. Wake up with a new focus and perspective that both challenges and celebrates you. Change is never easy, time is short, and distractions will always be around us, but despite all of this, opportunities are endless and you can do this for you.

CHAPTER 2

Identify the want or need. Ask yourself, "What?"

> What?" is a powerful question! I believe what is a driving force around the things we set out to do. The goals we want to achieve, the things we strive to accomplish or the dreams we hold for ourselves come through asking "What?" The question "What?" can lay the foundation to the plans we set for our lives.

Read through that first paragraph again. What do you want? What do you need? You might have heard this a number of times throughout life about identifying your needs and wants. I am asking you to look seriously at both questions. I think sometimes we see wants and needs in terms of material possessions, but I think it's important we also look at them in terms of what we want to achieve in life and what we need to help us, whether it be building relationships, creating partnerships or something in between. To get to where we want to be we might just need to take a more in-depth look at what we need.

Asking "What?" can lay the foundation to our future. A strong foundation can allow for the building of a successful future full of endless opportunity. The way in which we get there will vary person to person, but the question will remain the same: what do you want to do with your life? What are your goals? What do you want to accomplish? What will you need to help you get there?

Many people don't know what they want or need because their view keeps changing depending on circumstances in life. While it is always important that we take in what is going on around us, it is important we don't allow that to impact too greatly who we want to become and the changes we want for ourselves. Don't let your current circumstance or situation dictate who you want to become. While circumstances will change, and needs or wants will also, don't allow your happiness or satisfaction to depend entirely on a circumstance, because situations will change throughout our lives.

Be real with yourself and who you want to become. There is much to be achieved. Opportunities will come and go and circumstances will change, but you should hold strongly to who you want to become as you navigate

Identify the want or need. Ask yourself, "What?"

through life. Those changes shouldn't deflate you, they should help you to shine.

Far too many times in life people get stuck, stop, and start again on something new. While there is nothing wrong with starting again, I believe in life we achieve far less than what we are capable of simply because we don't modify the "What?" as we move through life. What we want to do at age 25 will look far different than what we want to achieve at age 50. It does not mean we were not meant to achieve the same thing, but the "What?" might be slightly different. I believe our needs change as we go through life also. What we want and what we need will be different as we grow older.

For example, I thought I would have three children. I would have one at 25, another at 27, and the last at 29. Well, the "What?" changed in my life because of other things. My first was born at 29 and my second at 31. I had two children, not three. My plans changed in life and I had adjusted my "What?" It didn't mean I was unhappy, but I ended up starting my career a little later in life and then purchased a home. This was what I wanted to do, and through it I tweaked other parts of my life.

What if you are closer than you think to achieving your goal? Have you stopped and looked at how far you are from where you want to be? Often we beat ourselves up more than we choose to see the growth. Have you actually taken the time to reflect on yourself? If not, you should take time to do so. If you have, then what did you see? In life, we have each made some sort of progress. We had things we couldn't do as an infant: we learned to walk or talk, etc. As a teen we could do more than as a child. There again was progress.

There is something you are able to do now, that at one time you might have not been able to do so easily. What is that? Take time to think about it. Then measure that against where you want to be. Choose to identify the progress, start there and move ahead. You are closer to your goal than you think. Reimagine the possibilities for yourself. It may involve a slight change to what you are trying to go after.

What are your feelings about this particular goal? Is it something you are passionate about or something you feel strongly about? Is it something you feel you must do or would like to do? These are great questions to ask yourself as you begin to identify your goals. The feelings produced by asking these questions might be key in focusing in on what you want for yourself and the changes that will be necessary for you. Take time to actually picture yourself meeting that which you are working towards, and all the time and effort you put towards your goal and the feeling created when you achieve it.

What is challenging you from moving forward? What is it that makes you want to change, but keeps holding you back from taking that first step? Is it the thought of having to do things differently than you have had to do before? Is it confusion over where to begin, to the point of choosing not to begin at all? If so, just start somewhere. If you're wrong, start again. You are making a change. This is not supposed to be an easy path. There will

Identify the want or need. Ask yourself, "What?"

be points you stumble or take a wrong turn, but you push forward anyway. There will also be moments where you see your progress and hit your highs. Those are the moments you are going to keep working towards. Begin somewhere. If you are wrong in how you start this decision it is up to you, not anyone else. In fact, no one really needs to know the details of your path to making a change. They will simply see the change themselves as you go along.

As you work to develop your goals, what can you learn in the process? Take time to stop along the way and think not simply about how you can gain more knowledge, but what you can identify more about yourself as you go through the steps and process of setting your goals. When I started my business, I learned a tremendous deal about how to begin a business.

I also learned more about the drive within myself. I took slow steps outside of my comfort zone. This was no easy task! I'm more of an introvert by nature. The thought of starting my own business was a large project. One that I thought was beyond my ability. I needed to do a lot of research to set everything up. I needed to push myself at times to reach beyond what I thought I was able to do. You will need to dig deep at times and find the drive within yourself to complete the tasks you set for yourself.

From creating a Facebook page to setting up my first website, I learned so much about the process and myself. This is where my mental focus needed to kick into overdrive. At times I would find myself thinking negative thoughts like, "I can't". I needed to fight through those negative poor self-confidence moments and be stronger than my thoughts. I needed to keep preparing myself to take that next step. When I took a wrong turn,

I needed to redirect my focus and my energy to the fact that I still could do this and I simply needed to find another way. About four years later and I'm still doing the same thing, and guess what?!? I started another business.

I didn't fail. I thought of another way. Another way to reach others and do more for myself in the process. I'm 38 and have started two businesses, published two books with another in the works, and have had some career re-directs. I didn't fail, I refocused. I took a harder road. I tried something new. I changed direction and challenged myself. Sometimes taking a step in a new direction isn't missed opportunities, but simply new possibilities. I write this to share with you that you can do this! I learned more about myself. I redefined what I wanted in my life. What I wanted to learn and ultimately do. People might have criticized my choices, and they might well do the same for you, but this is your journey. Always hold that deep within your heart and fresh in your mind. Remember when I said what you want and what you need will change in life? Keep changing

> You need to focus on the positive. Keep looking at progress, not perfection.

with it. Keep identifying what you want for yourself. Learn to embrace the changes in life, especially when it comes to you. What can you learn? I challenge you to ask yourself, "What can I do for me?"

What happens today and what happens tomorrow will be completely different. What you do as a result is up to you! You can keep moving ahead. You need to focus on the positive. Keep looking at progress, not perfection. Tomorrow may throw the unexpected our way, but we cannot let it derail us. Progress is more realistic than perfection. While it is always

Identify the want or need. Ask yourself, "What?"

good to strive to do your best, it is most important that you be your best! Perfection can at times take our focus off what we have accomplished and who we have become.

It is always important we keep our lives well rounded. What comes your way doesn't have to defeat you, it can define you. Allow the things that come your way to strengthen you, not set you back. Perfection can make us compare ourselves with one another. It isn't necessary to do this to ourselves in life, because it tears us down. It can make us feel inadequate and at times unqualified. How are those feelings going to lead you to want to change? They are more likely going to make you tend to want to throw in the towel and give up on what you are trying to do for you.

I might not be on any best seller book list in my life, and maybe I will, but I don't make that my purpose in being an author. For me that would be an added bonus in my life. I make it the lives I can impact in some way, the people I can help along the way, or the changes I make within myself through my focus. Daily life will always be, but we must be focused enough to look ahead at all there is for us that we can do.

We are made to achieve great things in life. Many times I think we feel we fall short when in all actuality we did not. What we want to achieve is within our grasp. To make a change, we must ask ourselves what it is we want. We must take a deep look at what it is we truly want for ourselves. What is it that we are striving for? What is it that will make us feel a sense of accomplishment? What will create a more well-rounded lifestyle for us and allow us to grow throughout our life. Is it family, friends, building relationships, etc.?

What are the lessons you learned along the way? This is another big question we must ask ourselves in order to identify the change we want. This is something that you might have to dig deep and really process. You might start by finding the area you want to make the biggest change. What area do you find you keep trying to tweak in your life? Often there are multiple areas, but start in the area you are willing to commit to long term. Then you can look at ways you can shape other areas also. You might even find through the one, that others link together. Through making the one change, other changes might be easier to set in place.

Look at the area that you may have been trying repeatedly at, but feeling like you haven't quite made a change. What did you learn each time you went through your experience? Was it the same thing every time, or did you pause long enough to reflect on the bigger picture? There is a lesson in every experience. What the lesson is for you will look much different than what it will look like for me, but we all share the same experience of learning lessons through each thing we encounter in life. It might be a short lesson, or it might be a more emotional, in-depth experience. Whatever the case, I believe each experience holds some kind of take away we should stop and identify.

We say we don't have a lot of time in life, and while that may hold true, this is an important thing for us in which we need to make time for. Lessons are an important experience in life. It is the lesson that can help shape the journey. Through the lesson, we might learn more about ourselves and the way we want to plan for our lives. If we don't really get ahold of the lesson learned, we might spend our lives incorrectly shaping what it is we want.

Identify the want or need. Ask yourself, "What?"

Always striving, but never really feeling like we got a hold on that which we are working towards. We may even find ourselves stopping short and restarting only to end up going in the wrong direction because we never really identified what went wrong or could have been slightly changed in the first place. It is the lesson that can both challenge us and move us in ways we never thought possible. It is the "What?" that helps shape the way we learn, grow, and reach for things in life.

Once you have thought about the lesson learned, you can then work on focusing on what change you might want to make moving forward and what you will need to get there. These can help create a solid foundation for you to build upon. A way to set yourself up to be more successful in reaching what you are looking to achieve. In making the change you want to for yourself.

Through looking at the change we want to make within ourselves or the goals or dreams we hope to achieve in life, we should think about the steps we need to get there. Many times we create something we want to achieve, and I think if we're honest we set the bar for ourselves too high. Let's take a weight loss goal as an example. If I say I want to lose weight and I want to lose 100 pounds, I think it is important to create smaller steps to achieving that goal. This must be broken down into smaller steps, otherwise you might become overwhelmed and think you have to be at a certain point faster than is either possible or than you need to be. We might just give up when this goal is achievable, but we set the bar too high. We will take a more in-depth look at the process and importance of creating steps later in the book, but this is something to think about as you answer the question about what you want. I know many times in my life I have set a weight loss goal only to achieve some part of it and begin to backslide when I could have just as easily maintained.

The same goes for many areas in our life. If we set too many goals, or we don't really narrow down our focus, we become overwhelmed and might even lose sight of any progress we have made. A question we should also ask ourselves is, "What is one way I can make my life less stressful?" This is a great way to create change in our lives through making one small change. Taking one thing off of our list can help us refocus and at times rebalance our lives. What is that one thing in your life? Sometimes we get so busy we forget to take the time to look at one thing we might be able to do to de-stress our lives.

Asking what the short-term and long-term goals are in different areas of our life is another thing to focus on. We can choose to make many of our goals long term, but I think it is important to have short-term goals to keep ourselves on track, feel a sense of accomplishment, and continue our drive to push forward and see results. Short-term goals create a sense of achievement in our lives and can be the building blocks to greater things. They also can create a feeling of fulfillment within our lives.

As we go through our lives it is important to keep looking at what it is we want. How often you choose to reflect upon this is up to you, but the more frequently you do, the fresher it will be in your mind. You can create the life you want for yourself and make the necessary changes you decide to make. Don't lose sight of what you are looking to accomplish. If you have a setback in an area, ask yourself again what it is you want and need.

Identify the want or need. Ask yourself, "What?"

Take the necessary steps to refocus on you. You will not regret the time you took for yourself in life to create the change you wanted to see within your life.

We might have to ask ourselves what we want or need many different times throughout our journey as we encounter new things. This is key to identifying the direction we take for ourselves in life. New direction doesn't mean we missed out on something or did anything wrong. It might simply be a redirect of our wants and needs in life. I have heard it said that your taste changes in life as you get older. I believe the same can be said about the vision for your life as you get older. Your focus becomes different. When you are younger you might see more of the broader picture, but as you get older you might find you are more focused on the details in the moment. Your focus will change as you redirect your life. What was once so important to you might not be 10, 20, or even 30 years down the road. The lessons learned in life can also shape that which we want to become even more.

> Your focus will change as you redirect your life. What was once so important to you might not be 10, 20, or even 30 years down the road. The lessons learned in life can also shape that which we want to become even more.

Keep your curiosity going. Think for a minute about a child and how they simply want to explore life. They are always seeking to learn. Did you ever stop and observe how they are always seeking to do more? They always share their wants, and they continually want more. They often say, "I want", "I want", "I want", and then, once given that one thing, they move on to the next. Overall, they transition well in different areas of life.

Perhaps it's their curiosity or maybe that they are not bogged down by the weight of the world. Make that yourself also.

The world will always compete in some way for our focus. Don't allow the world to drain you of your energy and belief in yourself. Have that childlike curiosity for your future. Always wanting more. Always asking why. Always seeking to learn more. Did you ever notice how children don't feel the need to impress anyone the way teens or adults seem to feel the need to? They seem to be unimpressed by competing with others. They simply live in the moment.

Ask yourself what the steps will be in the process toward the change you want to make as well. Identify them, but do so loosely, knowing they will also change as you move forward. I think of how a baby learns to walk from crawling. They don't instantly get up and walk. They stagger or perhaps stumble and may fall occasionally, but they get up and try again. I think the same must be said for ourselves as we make change and transition in our life. We may stumble or perhaps fall, but readjust the pace and see if that helps you better. That might be key in getting into a new rhythm for yourself.

I also think of a child learning to ride a bike. Some children might take days and others might take minutes, but they still keep working towards it. Some might need to take a break and begin again, or some might need a more creative approach, but they eventually get to their goal. What is the key? I believe it is that they keep working towards it. The same can be said for us. Keep working towards it and you can get there. The funny thing in life is that, once you learn to ride a bike, you can go years without riding

Identify the want or need. Ask yourself, "What?"

one again, but once you do you will once again remember how. What if we took that same approach to our goals? Take a break, but remember them. Think of a new way if that works as well, but go back to them. Sometimes it is all in our approach. We all learn in different ways and in different timeframes. Remember that as you move forward. It might just be the motivation you need at times to keep working at something.

Ask yourself what you want and why, and take more time to live in the moment. Just be you. If we feel we need to be anyone other than ourselves, our drive and focus in life become consumed by other things. Don't let other people make you want to become anyone other than yourself. We are all unique. We should strive to make changes in our life, but not in order to be anyone other than ourselves. As I think more to how children don't seem pressured to impress others but to simply be and explore, I think about how that is important to our lives also.

Explore your life. Explore your opportunities. Always want more for yourself. Always keep asking questions along the way. Always ask what you can do to change your life in a positive way. Always want more for yourself and your life. Live your hopes and dreams. Create the steps of your journey to be exciting. Challenge yourself to learn more and grow more. There is an exciting journey for you on your way to your destination. Change doesn't have to be scary, it can be fun. Don't get caught up in the drama we call life. Drama can bog you down and leave you with a feeling of defeat. Those feelings won't make you feel motivated to change. Always ask "Why?" and let your passion and the changes you can make, allow you reach new levels in life.

Make time for yourself. It is important to carve out the time you need to identify what you want to do in your life. You cannot keep pouring out and expecting to be refreshed and refocused enough to push ahead for you. Something in life will suffer as a result. What do you need to do for yourself? What might doing more for yourself look like? Maybe it is setting aside some time each week to plan. Whatever it is, don't sacrifice the time for doing for yourself. Progress is made one step at a time. Each step we take we need to remind ourselves to stay focused on the "What?" and not easily get lost and lose sight of that which we want for our lives.

Something eye-opening for me happened when someone once asked me what I did for fun. I couldn't quite answer that, which got me thinking more about life and the need to do more for myself. It made me think about the importance of adding fun to our lives to make life more exciting and real for ourselves. I had someone also ask me what I did for myself. I struggled with finding an answer for that also, as I had been so engrossed in being a mom and in simply doing the things that were necessary in life. I had to seriously stop and think about adding both of these elements, in some small way, to my life. You can do the same for you. We all can add things to our lives and should not feel guilty about adding change for ourselves.

CHAPTER 3

Why, Why, Why...

The "Why?" is what we need to identify behind asking the "What?" in our lives. Why did we identify a certain task, idea, etc. as something we wanted to accomplish? Why is that important to us? When we take time to pause and think about the "Why?" behind what we do in life, we might find we take the necessary steps needed to accomplish that goal or task in a new way. It might sharpen the lens of our perspective to achieving a more detailed plan for ourselves and our life.

By looking at and really focusing in on the "Why?" we will be able to create a more detailed structure to which we can build upon the foundation of the "What"? If you have ever stopped to really reflect and ask yourself why you have done something, it might either make you rethink your steps

4 Ways to Make a Change

and identify more with your needs and take a pause, or drive you forward in a new direction.

If I want to make a change in my life, I should ask, "Why do I want to make that change? Why do I feel I need to make that change?" As we get older in life, we might really find we look at the "Why?" more frequently than we once did. The "Why?" is like a pillar for what we do in life. You might even find you made a mistake and the question naturally flows, "Why did I do that?" The answer only you will know, but it is important you identify the "Why?". Identifying the "Why?" could lead to a change in thought, emotion, or direction in your life.

> As we get older in life, we might really find we look at the "Why?" more frequently than we once did. The "Why?" is like a pillar for what we do in life.

Through asking ourselves "Why?", different emotions can be experienced. "Why?" is a question that has many different responses. It is also one that can lead us to go in a new direction. It can be the fuel we need to make the necessary change or changes in our life to building the life we want to live, taking a step back and learning new ways to redirect our focus.

For instance, why do we constantly start and stop things in life? Take new year's resolutions for example. How many times do we start out by saying this is what I am going to do and get a month or so into it and stop? Is it because we are fearful of challenge and change? I think this is a greater possibility than we realize. I think maybe it is the element of the unknown and moving past it. Those "What if?" questions creep into the picture and we stop short of attaining something simply because we fear a possibility

Why, Why, Why…

that might never be. Stop thinking of the "What if?" and start moving toward the possibility. The possibility that you can change. The possibility that you can succeed. The possibility that you were made to do great things in life. The possibility of creating a greater future for yourself and doing more for you!

Why do we fear the unknown so much? Have you ever stopped to really think about this? There are many things that we start and stop in life, but why do we give up, or simply not finish? We are all in on a change we want to make or goal we set, and then we don't complete it. Is it the fear of something new and getting started that makes us either put it off or decide not to do it? Perhaps it is the fear of not meeting our high expectations that make us give up. Maybe it could even be the fear of continuously needing to reach outside of our comfort zone. The possibility of someone else doing it better than us might also penetrate our minds to the point that we feel we aren't good enough and think twice about even continuing on.

> Why do we fear the unknown so much? Have you ever stopped to really think about this? There are many things that we start and stop in life, but why do we give up, or simply not finish?

I know I have encountered some of these along my journey. Do any of those reasons sound familiar for you? Well, let me tell you, today is a new day. Put those unknown fears aside, because they are just that: unknown. What if the possibility of success lay within reach for you? Would your thought patterns change if you could visually see success? I believe so. So, what is stopping you from visualizing your success every single day? Is it that unknown? Those fears are all in your head. Your mind creates the fears. Whatever those fears are, you visually set them for yourself and you can change those thoughts also.

Reprogramming our thoughts is something that will take work. It is necessary to face the fear of the unknown or any fears we place in our minds as we take steps forward in life. Each day we get up we have the opportunity to do more. It will take getting over fears in order to set in motion what we hope to accomplish. Why do we have such routines in our life? I believe routine provides comfort, where as change challenges comfort. It will take conscious effort on your part to face the "Why" of the fears you have set in your mind and getting past them. You are capable of making changes to your life, and you might have to start with "Why?" An example might be, "Why am I so fearful?" Do any of the questions about the unknown resonate with you?

Fears can lead us to exhaustion, I believe. We get ourselves worked up over situations or possibilities that might not even happen. We work ourselves up to be the best because we fear looking silly, stupid, or less than. We wear ourselves out trying to stay one step ahead, when we only need to stay in pace with our own steps. This change is about you, and life can only be lived once. Don't waste it with fears; live it with change! Change your thought pattern. This is difficult, but it can be achieved. The only thing that stands in the way is you. It is not by any means easy, but it is necessary to stop our own fears from disqualifying us in life. For far too long I did that, and it wasn't fun.

I don't know a lot about running a business, but I continue to learn more each day and with each step I take. I know more than I did three years ago

Why, Why, Why...

when it all started, and a year from now I will know a little bit more. This took a huge amount of goal setting, learning and pushing my fears aside a lot of the time. I am not afraid to ask questions, and I might ask too many at times, but it is key to learning. I don't fear looking stupid as much as I did before. Don't get me wrong: those moments do creep up, but I have to really work hard when they do to keep myself from allowing them to control the changes I want to set and make for myself.

Every day we get up we have a number of choices we have to make. One of those choices could and often does involve fear of the unknown. We don't know what the day will bring. If we did, we might choose not to get out of bed in the morning at times if we're honest, but how boring life would be if we knew everything. Have you ever really thought about that? Think about how much more exciting every day is as we walk through life. If you knew all the pieces of your life, it would be boring. That unknown actually pushes us forward through our day. How many times have you worked yourself up over a meeting, interview, test, or some other thing in life and afterward said, "Well, that actually went a lot better than expected." Think of the amount of time you wasted in fear or nervousness. Now think of a situation where you thought, "Oh that interview, meeting, etc. will be easy," and then - BAM! - something happens that you did not expect. I think many of us have had that happen, where we felt completely blind sided as a result of it.

Think of how much calmer you were going into the second situation than the first, right? I think a lot of that can be related to life also. How many times does that fear of the unknown plague our minds to the point that we don't relax and explore? Instead, we panic and quit when in actuality we have made some changes and have done a good job.

My point in this example is that it seems to happen a lot in our lives. We work ourselves up over something and the outcome ends up being extremely different than what we expected. Can you relate this also to how you are mapping out making a change in your life? Are you getting yourself worked up over something and fearful of making a change because in your mind you have created a list of possible scenarios in advance? What if you changed your approach and allowed yourself the opportunity to reprogram your thoughts, to thinking more about how smoothly the change can be for you - thinking that you can achieve it?

Why don't you visualize the progress you can make and the positive things that can happen as a result? I think creating a visual that is possible and positive helps us to move against our fears and take the step forward. You might not necessarily have control of what happens at all times along the way, but you do have control over your thoughts and reactions to it as you go along the way. Each day, take even five minutes to visualize all that you can do in your life. Keep a journal or another way that works for you, but record your vision and your feelings. That could be the very thing that helps you when you are feeling weak.

If I would have allowed fear of the unknown to consume me, I would have never written my first book and explored the publishing process. As a result, this book would have never been. This is not the case. I explored what I wanted to do and I tried. You can try as well. You will feel better in life for having tried than for having wondered. That is something I can

Why, Why, Why…

tell you. I had zero idea about the process until I began to try and explore the possibilities. Do the same for yourself. The books I have written have been great at reaching some people out there. That in and of itself is rewarding to me. I hope this book will reach people as well, and encourage them to do more and reach for more in life.

I don't have any idea of the books I will write in the future or whether or not they will sell. I also don't know what my business will look like a month from now, let alone a year. I could focus on never being on a best seller list - or worse yet, not having a single copy sell - thinking about all the possible problems or other negative outcomes, but where would that get me? I know exactly where: fearful to move forward or feeling as though I should give up. Instead, I can choose to wake up each day imagining the many opportunities the day could bring, thinking more on the forward progress I will make. What I need to do is think of the change I would like to make and keep moving forward. The fear of "What if no one buys my books?" or the fear of various situations of growing my business need to be overlooked by focusing on the impact I can make and the fact that I can keep moving ahead.

The only other option is to work ourselves up over unknown situations or circumstances that we may never encounter and waste our energy and drive. Positive possibilities or negative unknowns. I'll take the positive possibilities, as they are more likely to get me more motivated to put one foot in front of the other. Positive preparation meets opportunity every time.

The opportunities are that which are going to fuel me to move forward. Think of the opportunities that can be a part of your future as well. Don't be fearful to take that leap forward. You owe it to yourself to reach forward and try. Making a change will bring a time of transition. Think of all the things that can go right.

A big part of making a change in our life involves taking out the negative. Negative thoughts, words, feelings, etc. have no place in your future. You can never fully prepare for the unknown, but you can choose your focus through it. Don't allow fear of the unknown to be your focus, or it will win every time! Don't put off making that change one more day because of it!

Why do you keep putting it aside? Oftentimes we put things off in our life, saying, "I'll get to it tomorrow." Did you ever stop to think you might not have tomorrow? How many tomorrows will it be before you decide not to make the change simply because you kept putting it off? I believe putting things off in life can create added stress in our life because the matter keeps looming over our heads. The thing you want to change in your life, whether because of doubt or fear, will keep looming until you decide to deal with it. Change is a way to do so.

I was 33 before I took the leap. I signed the contract and submitted my first book to be published. I thought and thought about it and wished and wished. Problem with wishing, is it doesn't go anywhere until you decide to make the change. At the same time, I took a career redirect and decided to make a change. I ended up shortly after deciding to begin the publishing journey. Talk about two large changes to make in life. Although at times I was discouraged, I continued to keep putting one foot in front of the other.

My "What" and "Why?" in this case changed in a very big and - if I am honest - scary way at times. The decision to take a step back in my career was very difficult. There were some challenges I made as I faced that decision. When I signed the contract to publish my book, I thought, "Here goes!" It was an overwhelming feeling as I thought about the process and steps that lay ahead for me. I have a friend who I bounce a lot of ideas off of. I remember calling that friend and sharing my decision with them. Wow! A career redirect and taking a chance on being a published author: a huge life change in a number of ways.

I can tell you I never would have been the person I am today if I hadn't decided to make the change. I did what was best for me. I advocated for myself in many ways and the changes I wanted in my life. My life has changed in many ways, in what I have accomplished and how I have felt about myself. I have been able to do things I initially would have never even tried. That step in my journey was very tough. I had to dig deep and keep climbing. I had to believe in myself and what I could do. I had to reach beyond my comfort zone in many ways. The experiences I encountered and the lessons I have taken away have allowed for growth and change that might have never been a part of my journey if I chose to simply be, never wanting a change in my life.

The unknown will always be, but the reason we push ahead should be greater than the "What if?" we try to create in our minds. Perhaps another reason why we give up on things so quickly is a lack of belief in ourselves. We create a checklist for our lives or our goals, and if we don't accomplish it the way we had hoped or envisioned, we give up rather than rethink the possibilities. As hard as it is, we need to stop this cycle at some point in our life and believe in ourselves.

If I come up with a list of ten things I want to get done today and only complete three, I don't think to myself, "Well let's throw the list away and just forget it." No, I look at the list and do one of two things. Either I break it down in smaller steps, or I try another day to accomplish them. Those things still need to get done; they just need to get done differently. Can you imagine what life would look like if we threw away every list we made because we didn't accomplish something? This is the same for the challenges you face. Don't throw your list away. Don't give up on yourself. Don't fear the change simply because things didn't go as planned when you started out. Break it down into more achievable steps for you or change your timeline for achieving your goal. Give yourself more credit: you are trying to make a change. Look at the things you have accomplished. At the end of our day, we still have a list of things we need to get done. During the times I don't get done what I want to, I still look at what I did get done. I think this is the same for change in our life. We still have change that we want to achieve and we need to look at the changes already made in order to motivate ourselves to continue on our way.

I believe "Why?" to be a very deep question. Think about something you wanted to achieve when you were younger: why has your viewpoint changed on that thing you wanted for yourself as you got older? Was there

Why, Why, Why...

a lesson learned? Something experienced that made you take a step forward, but in a slightly new way? Did you give up for some reason, stopping short of achieving that which you sought to do because of an emotion? Is that something you still want for yourself? Look at how close the want is to the "Why?" The way we make a change might be hard, but it is important we ask ourselves "Why?"

Could the reason why you might not be starting, or you might be quitting more often, possibly be linked to comparison with another individual? Let me tell you: STOP RIGHT THERE!!! You are not them and they are not you! Each day we get up we have the ability to make a change. Each and every day! One change should be the way we see ourselves. Sometimes we feel inadequate, but does that feeling come about because of unnecessary pressure we place upon ourselves? I think most of the time if we're honest the answer to this question is, "Yes".

The answer: stop doing it! The reality? It's hard to do. This is done through steps as well. We must work at the way we view ourselves. For years I would compare myself with others, and at times I still tend to do this. What do they have that I lack? Does it really matter in the long run? Am I being the best version of myself through asking what someone else has that I do not? Not at all. It is not healthy for our lives. There is a lot I am qualified to do in life. That should be my focus. When I get off course and tend to look at what I feel I lack in comparison to what someone else I feel has, I get both discouraged and off course, both of which are going to prevent me from making progress to my goals or having motivation to change.

4 Ways to Make a Change

This is one of the "Whys?" that we must constantly work at. The world is full of competition. I think we create such added stress upon ourselves because of this. This change is not for them, it is for you. It should not be a change in order to be more like someone else. To have their qualities, their abilities, their talent, whatever else you see as lacking in you that someone else has. It's okay to want to have qualities that someone else does, but to do so in a manner that creates constant feelings of inadequacy within ourselves is simply not healthy. I did this far too often in my life and it was honestly not fair to me. I am me. I need to start with being okay with me. Trying to change ourselves to the point of being like someone else hides your true self. It hides your uniqueness, because we all are different. We all are unique in some way.

Why would you want to make a change to be someone else? I think that would become exhausting. Life is so short; never spend your time wishing you were someone else. It is a waste of your time. How is that productive to growing yourself in anyway? You can make a change. You can create a beautiful life for you by simply celebrating your abilities, talents and character. Look at all the traits you hold and work on shaping those, but don't criticize them because of someone else. You can grow and you can change. Spend life growing into the person you want to be through growing those unique talents and abilities.

> You can create a beautiful life for you by simply celebrating your abilities, talents and character.

While we might not know immediately why we want to make a change, we do know there is some reason why we keep circling around the feeling

30

Why, Why, Why…

of wanting or needing to do so. As we take steps toward meeting our goals, there will be reasons why we stop. If we do stop, it is important to look at that reason or reasons as well. Wants change, needs change, and with them, goals change.

The way to make a change is through constantly reflecting on our lives. We can set out to do something, but we must keep it fresh in our minds, otherwise we risk losing focus and becoming discouraged. Going back to my example of wanting to lose 100 pounds, why do you want to do that? Your answer to that question can create an in-depth look at yourself and your life. Why you want something will be different than other people. That must be carefully reflected upon, for that will help you as you push forward. Why do you want this for yourself? Why does that matter to you? Or another question for yourself if you made progress and had a setback might be, "Why did I backslide? I have oftentimes done this when trying to achieve a weight loss goal, or healthier eating plan in my life. The reason you identify as having backslid, might be just what you need to refuel and refocus to get moving again before you choose to give up.

Why dwell in the past when you can create such a great future? We all have had times where we have faced a missed opportunity or when we wish we had done something different. Don't dwell there! Don't waste your time wishing something were different; spend your time planning for what can be! Be excited about your future and don't live in the "Whys?" of the past. Identify them, but don't dwell in them. You can't change anything that happened. What you can change is how your journey will end. Make it real, make it exciting, make it about you!

I can think of a number of times in my life I gave up too soon. I didn't pause or reflect, I just said, "I am done". I didn't really give things the proper time I should have. Whether it was frustration, feeling overwhelmed, or a combination of both, I didn't weigh things out the way I should have. I didn't collect my thoughts and refocus my energy on a different attempt at that which I was working on. I simply gave up and quit. I took many valuable experiences away from having done so. I once had a time where I started over in a job I held. I chose to take a step down. For many years I thought I had failed. I went through the rebuilding process and fought through change in my life. I became a stronger, more well-rounded person because of my experience. I stepped out of my comfort zone more and grew as a person. I became an author and learned many valuable lessons about what I could do. Through your experiences, what have you learned about yourself?

See how important it is to take time for ourselves. To pause, reflect, and refocus at different times throughout our life can create the energy needed to move ahead in our journey. Don't lose sight of the reason why you want to make the change. There is powerful emotion and drive behind that reason. The reason why we want something is the reason why we do more for ourselves. The reason why we do things in life often has some sort of feeling or emotion behind it. Don't be afraid to identify what that is. Go all in with taking a deeper dive into your life.

> To pause, reflect, and refocus at different times throughout our life can create the energy needed to move ahead in our journey.

Why, Why, Why...

This is your life. Live each day with passion seeking every opportunity to grow, change and enjoy what lies ahead for you.

Learning to identify the "Why?" behind the "What?" is the thing in life that can help us to stop feeling stuck and to move forward. The identification of the "Why?" can be a difficult thing, but as you narrow down your focus you can then start to create steps to getting to where you want to be. It might not be something that comes instantly to mind, but it is a question you should ask yourself as you seek to make a change in your life. You can reach your goals. You can get to your destination. You can learn why it is you want something in life and really fuel yourself to making it happen for yourself.

> You can reach your goals. You can get to your destination. You can learn why it is you want something in life and really fuel yourself to making it happen for yourself.

4 Ways to Make a Change

CHAPTER 4

How am I going to get there?

There are many different things you can identify with "How?" The big question will be: how are you going to get to what you want to do or achieve? This question is a big one because it is up to you to determine your steps. It is up to you to push yourself to get there. The drive is in the way this question is answered. Often times it is through asking "How?" that we are pushed beyond our comfort zone.

Did you ever think, "How on earth am I ever going to achieve this?" You know how you're going to do it: through small steps and believing in yourself. That is how you are ultimately going to make the change. You know the best part about this is that you set the steps. Don't feel overwhelmed. Feel excited!

> You need to create your drive through stepping out of your comfort zone. The "How?" will challenge you. It can push you outside of your comfort zone in ways you never thought possible.

Did I just say that phrase…comfort zone? Yes. You need to create your drive through stepping out of your comfort zone. The "How?" will challenge you. It can push you outside of your comfort zone in ways you never thought possible. It doesn't have to be a large push to immediate, drastic action, but instead can be small steps to create a better you. Through reaching out of our comfort zone we learn a lot more about ourselves and feel empowered to do more in our lives. Once we feel a small accomplishment, I believe in some small way our emotion takes over and we want more of that feeling.

It is often hard to reach outside our comfort zone. Think about how much you will change as a result of doing so. It's pretty amazing at times how even the simple things can challenge us, but what great feeling we experience oftentimes after having done them. Keep your focus on the change, not the challenge. The challenge may paralyze us, but the change can amaze us. Live your life to amaze yourself. Live your life in such a way that you always want to identify how you are going to get to where you want to be.

Every day is a new day in which to create how you are going to achieve something. The really awe-inspiring thing is you get to create that "How?" every day of your entire life. What are you going to make it look like for you? There are many "How's?" that will align with your goal. If I decide today that I am going to change careers, I need to think about how that is

How am I going to get there?

going to evolve in my life. The steps might be short term, or they may be long term, depending on what I am choosing to do.

Does that career change involve an education? How long will I need to go to school for? How much money will it cost? How will I pay for it? How am I going to need to adjust my schedule? How will I balance this? How will it impact my life? These are some of the many questions that stem from looking at changing that one aspect of my life. If you are thinking about retirement, that is another big change, one that must be carefully aligned with goals and planned out.

How we go about getting to the next step is up to us, but I think it is important that we identify with ways that will move us. Not just physically, but in all areas of our lives. Ways that will challenge us and promote growth. Ways that in the end will be the change we wanted and were striving for within ourselves. No matter how big or small the change, it will be a change. Start small and grow larger. Set the "How?" Remember to set what is achievable for you. I am going to go back to my weight loss example again. How you get there is up to you, but make it stretch and move you in ways that will amaze even yourself. Remember: this journey is about you. Don't stretch to impress others; create your "How?" for you!

A puzzle comes together one piece at a time, and the changes you want to make do the same. Each piece is uniquely shaped in a configuration interlocking together to complete the puzzle. One piece locks into another to create a larger picture in the end. Your life is uniquely shaped as well. Each curve a turning point. Each edge a story.

4 Ways to Make a Change

Whether it's 500 or 1,000 pieces, the pieces all get put together one at a time over a length of time. You discover things as you put each piece in place. The colors, patterns, shape and design emerge as you progress further and further. The same can be said about the steps of your journey over the course of change in your life. It's done one step at a time. The landscape, view, and perspective often will change along with it.

Don't forget the many pieces, as they all hold value. As you continue on your journey, think about how each step doesn't have to be the same. Don't make changing your life more complicated or rigid, or you will never have fun and enjoy the life you are trying to create for yourself. If our steps are too big, readjust them if you must do so, but don't give up on yourself. Your journey will be filled with ups and downs, but it is the passion behind the change that will make you keep that fire within you strong.

Things in life are not achieved in one day. Remember that. No one can map out your future except you. You create the goals, you set the plans, you take the steps. It is all about you. Change can be extremely difficult, so make "How?" you are going to get there a way that does not frustrate you. Make it a way that you can feel good about yourself. A way that you can build up your self-confidence and self-esteem.

By the way, you are never too old to make a change. That book you want to write: do it! Let me write it again: you are NEVER too old to make a change in your life. In fact, that book you may want to write will be filled with experience because of your journey. Think about the impact you can make both on yourself and someone else through sharing your experiences. Think of your own growth. Maybe you have thought about going back to

How am I going to get there?

school. You are never too old to learn something new. Remember when I said wants or needs will change as you go through life? Explore all the options that are available to you and for you. Never stop looking ahead. Don't look behind and wish, look ahead and do! Something you wanted many years ago can still be attained; it might simply look slightly different to you than it once did. It does not mean you were never meant to change something in your life, it could be you were meant to do so in a completely different and unique way.

If I think about all the times I wanted something exactly the way I did and it didn't work out and look now at all I have achieved, I really believe it has made me a stronger, more well-rounded person for having gone on the journey I have. My "What?" changed many times along the way. In 2015, I wanted to write a children's book and be an author. I never initially wanted to start my own business, but then I did. My wants changed as I went through the process of being an author. My needs changed also, as I found I needed to start a business to sell some of my books.

How will you create the steps you want to achieve? That is the question you should start with. What is something that comes naturally to you? Maybe you should begin there. This way you have a place to start from. Remember, this should also challenge us a little in some way. Something that we can measurably achieve in some way. For example, maybe if you have a financial savings goal, you can start with one dollar a week and build it up from there. Maybe it's buying one less latte a week. Whatever it is, remember to not set the bar too high to begin with. You want to make sure you feel progress. For when we feel progress we can see change and with change growth.

Keep your mind focused on what is ahead. How you are going to get there is up to you, but add creativity to your canvas, a storyline to each page in your journey. If you do not add some sort of creative element, your journey will run the risk of becoming routine. Although through repetition we learn, repetition can make our lives less exciting as well. Doing the same thing over and over may lead us to becoming bored or to getting too comfortable. If we become too comfortable with something, we may not be as excited. We may also become less apt to reach out of our comfort zone and discover more about ourselves. The ability to reach for more lies within our grasp.

Change in life is never easy. Changing our own lives we may find especially hard. The way we make the change is our opportunity to share our creativity with the world. Let it move you, let it drive you, let it make you shine. Focus on the steps and what lies ahead. That which lies ahead is another "What?" that we must observe in our lives. Each step we take in our lives is a way to redefine how we are going to get to where we want to be. Every day we are given multiple opportunities to enrich our lives in so many ways. The "How?" can be defined every day. We choose the way in which we will get to our destination. We control the pace and how the steps are set. Life will always change around us, but the "How?" can only change through us, by our focus and determination to both set and reach our goals.

A large portion will be your focus. Your mental mindset and your physical drive. Each day we can make an impact on our future. Each day

How am I going to get there?

is a day to make progress. We must not define ourselves by the mistakes of the past, we must seek the opportunities of the future. If we define ourselves by the mistakes of the past, we will get lost in them, never getting past them with a new future in view. Each day is that future. Live it with passion and purpose and you will soar. That blank canvas will have many marks, but let them be ones of opportunity and purpose rather than defeat or discouragement. Get up again and again to keep creating.

Live life each day to create, not in chasing the past. Let the masterpiece of your life be made through creativity and passion. Through pressing through the challenges and choosing to see the change. When things don't quite work out the way you planned, don't wallow in the past; create a better, stronger future for yourself. We have 24 hours in each day in which we can create the very opportunity for ourselves that we so desire. That change we want to see.

> Live life each day to create, not in chasing the past. Let the masterpiece of your life be made through creativity and passion.

How will you measure your progress along the way? I think it is important we always have some sort of visual to remind ourselves of what we are working towards. This visual should be something we constantly review. Whether it be in the morning when we get up and are getting ready, or in the evening as a reflection, it is important we set a visual for ourselves. Sometimes journaling is a great idea, as it can help you to process your emotions and walk through the steps you are taking. You can also look back at your journey to see your pitfalls and your progress along the way.

Another question you can ask yourself through this process is, "How is the achievement of this going to make me feel? Identifying the way we will feel is another thing that will push us to move forward and take that next step. It runs alongside "Why?" Identification of our feelings in trying to make the changes we want to see in ourselves and our lives is a huge determination in how far we will go.

Feelings are an important thing to identify with. They can either drive us forward or paralyze us in fear. They can either make us determined to reach our goals or get stuck in the setback and not move ahead. Don't get stuck. Find out how you want to get to where you want to be, and be determined.

Along with asking ourselves the way in which we are going to get there, we should reflect upon our feelings. How will the accomplishment of this make me feel? Remember, feelings are often a powerful driver in what we do in life. How I feel today about something may change tomorrow, but it is important to keep at the forefront of our minds the way the achievement of this goal will make us feel so we keep ourselves motivated on our way to achieving it.

We might have days when a setback does arise, but remember, that is just one day. There are many days ahead for you as you work towards your goal. I think it is important if we experience a setback that we view it as a stepping stone on our path. A time to pause and take in all we have accomplished and to remember that. Small steps create larger leaps in life. Remember: you are trying to reach out of your comfort zone to stretch

How am I going to get there?

yourself and grow. This takes a lot of strength at times as we put aside our fears or other feelings and move ahead.

Be proud of even the small ways that you have attempted to reach for more, and keep focused on your potential. Remember, our lives are like a canvas. Each day is an opportunity for a fresh idea, a new stroke of the brush.

Don't give in to the negative self-talk. How you will get to where you want to be will bring about challenges. Be determined to overcome them. Change is never easy, but how we get to where we want to be is a lifelong process. With each step of progress, be determined to reach for more, identifying how next to get there. You picked up this book most likely because you wanted to make a change. How you make that change is up to you. How you create the steps and motivate yourself is up to you, but you must create the drive to do so. No one can do this for you; this is up to you and you can do this! You need to do this for yourself.

In identifying the steps of how you will get there, also identify how the people around you might be able to assist you with making a change. There might not be anyone as you first begin, but there might be someone who can help as you move ahead. The friend I mentioned before, they are able to provide that honest feedback and I appreciate it a lot. I have had times I have needed to take time to vent, or simply share my thoughts on a topic and be real, and it has been nice to have someone to be able to celebrate accomplishments or at times to correct me on a point, thought or idea to provide honest feedback. I consider them a valuable part of the changes I have made at various points in my journey.

4 Ways to Make a Change

Find someone who can assist you also to help you on your way. We all can use those people in our life we can trust to share with that we feel will also be honest. People who can support us and have seen our growth along the way. Someone who has seen how your journey has come along. It is tough to change, but support is a nice way of making it a little easier.

It is especially valuable to have someone who might be able to call out any faults you have or the directions you're heading that might take you way off course. Those are the people you should hold on to closely, especially as you strive to make any difficult changes along the way. That person I mentioned has been able to give me a lot of insight at various points. They have also been there to help me celebrate as I have overcome challenging moments to becoming more well-rounded in various areas.

How you will get there is also through fighting through any and all criticism that might tend to throw you off course. Some criticism is needed to help us, of course, but you need to carefully filter what you let in. There is criticism that will help us as we move forward, but there is also criticism that if we hold tightly to it will not lead to us seeking growth within ourselves. Choose wisely that with which you allow to filter through your mind.

We will not be perfect. We must simply do our best. At the same time, we need to be open to receiving some criticism. The time I took a career redirect and tried my hand at publishing were some of the most trying moments in my life. I had critics, I heard rumors that were said, information was not communicated in the way I thought it should have been, but I needed to try to focus on the change for myself through the challenge. I learned the importance of not looking for praise in life and that people will always have an opinion. This is something I still continue to remember as I go about my day and wanting to make even more changes in my life.

Change is hard enough, don't make it even harder by looking for praise in order to keep moving forward, because it won't always work out that way. It's important to remember you are building your future. There may be those who are considered favorites over you, or who are more critical, but don't let that cloud your focus. Always remember you are trying to do more for yourself. Don't seek change in your life so you can be added to a list of most qualified whether it be in school, a job, sports, etc. You are qualified to do many things. That is key to growth in many areas of life.

I think for a lot of my journey that piece was missing in my life. I would look at different areas and either disqualify myself or think I could not do a certain job or task simply because of other people. Another thing to remember is not to keep knocking on the doors that have closed, because you'll only end up with bloody knuckles. That door either did not or is not opening for a reason. Don't waste time trying to find out the reason. If it is something you did in the past, reflect upon what you learned and move ahead.

As you try new things remember that you will not be the best right off the bat. Sometimes we take off on different adventures in life and I think we expect more of ourselves than we ought. Sometimes our own expectations are higher than perhaps they should be for ourselves. Maybe it's that we look to where others are and rush. Whatever the case, make looking at how you will get there one of the focus areas as you map out the change you want to see and set for your life.

Don't miss out on the changes you can make in your life because you fear the difficulty. If you are afraid of your goal, it just may push you forward to prove to yourself all that you can do! Do it for you! You might be closer to that change than you ever thought possible. How best to get there is small steps. It doesn't matter how many steps it takes you to get to where you want to be. Just take it in stride. Strive for more. Small steps allow us to experience progress slowly and to take hold of the change we are experiencing in life. Small steps can also slow us down enough to not be as scared of the change we are trying to make in this fast and often crazy life we live in at times. Small steps can also allow us the opportunity to experience greater pauses and in turn greater growth.

Think of it like saving for retirement. I cannot put all of my money in today and retire tomorrow. I must put my money in over time in small steps to see growth. Today I might put in one percent and then go to two, but no matter what, in time it is going to grow. There are also investment options I might need to change as I get older as well. I might need to put less into stocks and more into bonds or less into one account and more in another. Think of your life that way as well. In time you will see that change and you will grow. Investing in ourselves takes time.

The thing you feel you cannot do today, set that thought aside, because you might be able to do it easily in the future. Don't allow that one thing to make you not even want to try. Tweak your goal or your approach and move ahead. This is something you have identified as a change you want

How am I going to get there?

to make. As you grow and move forward, your "How?" will change. As that changes you might even notice the very thing you feared doing is the thing you needed to do to create the greatest growth within yourself. Once you accomplished that, the steps might gradually become different. Taking the proper steps will lead to a greater feeling of accomplishment along the way. If we reach too far or if we try to do too much, it might create feelings of anxiety or discouragement.

As you set your goals, think of any obstacles you might face along the way as you work through the "How?", but by working through them you can only grow in some way. Runners don't see a hurdle and avoid it on the race, they see one and jump over it. We too can learn to do that in our lives as well. Go over the hurdles with ease as you create change and transition in your life.

Now, on to the fun part of this chapter: the last part of the "How?" is celebration! How are you going to celebrate what you are working to accomplish? I believe it is important to have celebration along the way in our journey to help both refresh and keep us excited about what we are looking to achieve. It allows us to look at the positive in our journey. It forces us to take a pause and look at our accomplishments. To celebrate ourselves! Did I just say "celebrate ourselves"? Yes. It is important that we celebrate what we do in life. That could be just what we need to fuel our hearts, minds, and bodies to keep moving forward. If we keep marching on, but don't take time to view the progress or celebrate, then we won't take the time to reflect upon the journey. By taking that pause to celebrate, we can experience the emotion and feeling of all that we have worked hard to do. Perhaps it's a day of fun, or simply an hour. The fact we reached for more in our lives, the fact that we made even the smallest of change, and that we grew in some way.

How you will celebrate is an important piece. This is your opportunity to implement doing something for yourself. Celebrating should be a large part of our lives. Our goals are a large part of who we want to become, and we should celebrate as we accomplish them. Maybe it's once a week, or once a month. Think about the reward behind each goal and perhaps even each step as you begin.

Really think about how you want to celebrate along the way, and reward yourself. This is the time to do for you! If we forget or fail to celebrate in life, our lives can become stagnant. If our lives become stagnant, we risk losing the ability to reach our full potential. How we are going to get there may be tough or seem scary, but don't lose sight of who you want to become or the changes you want to make. Only you can make them. The most exciting part of your journey can be the picture you will paint of your life. Each day is a new page in the chapter of our lives. Make the "How?" the most exciting chapter you will ever write.

How you will get there and how you will celebrate will be determined by you! How you break down the steps will also be determined by you. This is the time of breakthrough and change. This is the how that can be the first step of many for doing for yourself. Make it exciting, make it achievable, and make sure you celebrate!

CHAPTER 5

The When

The closing question is the "When?" When will you seek to achieve your goal or task by? If you are a planner by nature this might come easily; if you're not, planning this out might be very challenging. With the identification of when we want to achieve our goals by should also come the creation of the steps to get there. Ask yourself your long-term and short-term plans.

When we identify those, we can then fill in the steps of how to get there. When do you want to achieve that goal by? When we set smaller goals, we are more likely to build upon them to create a foundation for larger goals. When we make even small accomplishments, we want to keep moving forward. We should celebrate when we do these things.

If you are choosing right now as the time when you want to make that change, then what are the tools, resources, and steps you will need to reach your goal, dream, or task? You should work to identify those and jot them down somewhere. This will be a continuous reminder for you on your journey. If what you want to do is something you want to attain in the future, then you need to decide when that is and work to create a future plan. You can create your goals longer term. Perhaps your achievement of them might be more spread out. Think about the example of saving for retirement. We should put in little by little to fill our account. We should do that in our lives as well, investing little by little over the long term.

Maybe you're not exactly 100% percent sure of when you want to see this change. That's okay, but you should work to identify small things you can do to still move ahead anyway. This way it will keep your focus on what you want to do. That timeframe will also change depending on circumstances in life too.

Lastly, when you work hard, you will succeed. None of this will be possible without a commitment. That commitment must be one of determination. The journey will be hard, with difficult days. You will probably be tempted to throw in the towel more than one. That might just be a cue for you to slow down, take a pause, refresh you plan, and refocus. Don't allow yourself to quit something that you want to do for yourself, especially if you have tried in the past and given up. Now is your opportunity to see the positive within yourself. This is the time to stop and look at all you have achieved. Sometimes it's easier for us to give up than

The When

to push ahead. I know I have done this in my life more often than I would like to admit.

Some days we might not be feeling it, but don't let one day derail your progress. Many of us will experience an off day, but there is a difference between just having an off day and rethinking your entire journey. Don't let one down-in-the-dumps day throw off your entire journey. Recognize that the day is just an off day and reprogram your mindset. Remember: much of what we think we need to filter through the lens of truth when it comes to ourselves. A day we are not feeling it, is a day we really need to take greater effort to pull ourselves up. Those are the days we tend to pelt ourselves with "I feel less than" thoughts, when they should be days of rebuilding our mindset.

We can do this, and guess what?!? You are in it for a lifetime, so you need to make the best of any and all moments you have in life. Cry it out, take a pause and a breather, but don't give up! Life may be hard, but believe in yourself. Believe that this will improve in time. Breathe and take another step. Persevere. Don't lose sight of what you want for yourself because of how you feel about yourself one day. It is one day on the journey of a lifetime of change. If anything, stop on that day and ask yourself what happened and why you feel that way. Then figure out how you will keep moving forward.

When we do this, we set ourselves up for opportunity. Opportunity is a part of all of our futures. On days where you might not feel your best, always remember how much value you have to offer. Remember how this change will impact your life. Keep envisioning the success for yourself with any and all changes you make. We are all made to do great things. Great things start with you taking that first step toward change. Feed positive into your life. Great opportunities lie within each of our grasp. I cannot tell you the number of down days I have had, but how important it was for me to remember that it was one day of many on the steps of my journey. How I needed to pull myself up and remember what I was trying to achieve and do for myself. On the days where you might not be feeling it, lift your head and know you have a great future in store.

On the days where things don't make sense and you simply are caught off guard by what came your way, take another step. That's all I can say. It is hard, but not impossible. Be determined and dig your heels in. Tell yourself you are not going to quit on yourself. Tell yourself you have a journey you envisioned for yourself and you will get there. Take a walk, take a drive, but make sure at the end of the day you take another step forward. It might be in a new direction, but it will still be a step of progress nonetheless.

Today I was driving in a snowstorm to get to work. The roads were more difficult to navigate in some places than in others. Some spots I could go a little faster than others. As the maneuvering difficulty increased, I needed to slow down and focus harder on my driving to reach my destination. I needed to focus to stay on track and not slip off the road and spin out of control. There were spots that were slicker than others where I needed to be more cautious and aware.

The navigation throughout our life will change as well. Some spots we will need to navigate with more focus than others. Some distances will be

The When

longer, some turns sharper. We will encounter this as we strive to achieve our goals also. There will be messy parts to changing our lives as there were messy roads on my way to work.

The snowfall went on and off for a period of three days. I thought about how troubles in our lives can as well. How we have times where we coast along fine and then we get messy or slick portions. However, during the snowstorm we don't just stop our car in the middle of the roadway and leave. We make a choice of slowing down and focusing differently in the way we reach our destination. You could look at it like changing our approach because of the situation. By doing this we still reach our destination, just differently. If we apply this to making a change to our lives during the storm, we should slow down and refocus on our goal. This way we will still reach that which we are seeking.

Just like with the snowstorm, I still got to work, but it took me a little longer. My approach was different in that I left myself more time and I placed my focus on the roadway and slowed down. I was focused on the path to get me to my destination. Each bump, curve and slush of snow I had to be more aware of. They were problems in my life, but I didn't let them stop me. I simply needed to navigate differently through the difficulty. Think of the challenges to reaching your goals in the same way. You just need to navigate differently. Don't allow the difficulty to make you stop.

At times I feel we do not choose to slow down in life. Especially at times when we are working through our goals. Why is it that we don't? Only we can truly answer that. I think we try to reach for things too fast and become discouraged, when there might be a simple need to slow down and re-envision our goals. Just like in a snowstorm when we face challenges, we just need to take that time to slow down and refocus our effort. Effort can drain us if we spend it in the wrong areas, or by pushing too hard. This is where slowing down can allow us a moment to catch our breath. It can allow us to take life at our own pace rather than the pace life tries to set for us. The best part about this change is you get to be the designer. You set the time, you set the pace, you set the goal, and you are doing more for you in and through it all.

All of us wish we could have more things in life, and instantly. The fact that we live in such a fast-paced world doesn't help our situation at all. It is up to us to create the pace at which we will work to achieve our goals. It is up to us to set the time for ourselves. Fit the time into your situation and watch the results.

If you get a week or two weeks into your goal, don't give into the temptation to give up. You started this journey for a reason. You must remember that change takes time. Was your goal to eat healthier? Did you eat healthier the first or second week you started? If you made even one or two small changes, you made a change. How did it make you feel? Keep going back to that feeling. It will push and motivate you to keep moving forward. You made an attempt at a change. It takes time to get into a routine.

> If you get a week or two weeks into your goal, don't give into the temptation to give up. You started this journey for a reason.

Take some time to revisit what you are trying to change or the goals you are trying to set. Look back at when you started and why you either chose

The When

or are choosing to set that goal. What were you looking to achieve? How is your progress going? Then remember to recognize even the smallest accomplishment.

We also may need to refocus at different points. What might you be able to change to keep moving forward? Then look at why you think that change will help you and how this will help your short-term and long-term goal. Remember to write this down. Then look at ways to refresh the way you will begin or continue. How can you modify your goals and the reason or reasons why? A refresh can help our outlook sometimes tremendously.

Now you need to also remember to reflect on your progress! What worked well and what did not as you went about your goals or starting to change? As you look back, also think of why you chose to start on the path you did towards change or set the goals you had set. Look at also how you measured your progress and whether it worked for you. When we take time to reflect on things in life it can help us to rethink our steps or how we started and also about our progress. This can help us to move ahead. When we take small steps, we feel more accomplished. This can help us to achieve more for ourselves!

You must turn any negative energy into positive focus. Perhaps your "When?" must change. Learn how to take a step or two back, but try again. Don't stop there. You may have taken a wrong turn in your journey, but don't lose what was important to you. The change you want to make is possible. Many times, the only thing that stands in our way is our attitude. We might think we cannot do something, so we decide not to try. We spend a lot of our time wishing in life for that which we can actually achieve if we try.

You can do what you set out to do. The only thing that stands in your way is you. Take out the negativity. There is much in life you can work to achieve. That job you want to try for, do it! That book you want to write, try it! Begin somewhere. There are many lessons to be learned, but don't make the mistake of never learning them by never having tried.

This is your life, take the most time you can and do for yourself. Plan for your future and grow in doing so. Really take the time to look at these four questions and create the picture you want. Learn from the mistakes or the setbacks of the past. Investing in yourself takes time. It takes time to grow ourselves. To replace negative self-talk or feelings with positive motivation and determination. Ask yourself the hard reflective questions that only you can answer.

Don't allow your reason for making a change be solely to get recognition. You might not get it, or it might not be the way you were looking for it. Also, if we live our lives purely for recognition, each time we want to change our lives or meet a goal, then the highs in life might not outweigh the lows. We will most likely crash and be tempted to stay there. You might get the recognition in life, but I can say from my experiences in life, recognition is oftentimes short lived. Don't do this for approval or else you will become an approval addict, trying to be someone else when this is your life.

The world will always be looking for the next best thing. The next best diet, music, you name it. Don't fall into a trap. This change is about you!

The When

Each step you take is about you, not someone else. Someone once made the comment to me about having become an author and the instant reference to making money and quitting my job. Let me tell you, it doesn't work that way! I became an author because I wanted to do something that would change me and my life. I write for my love of writing, not for a steady paycheck. I write because I can encourage others. Becoming an author stretched my life and enriched it. It led me to reach for more, and to change myself. This was no easy task, and it isn't over yet!

I keep setting my goals, tweaking them as I see fit and learning more about myself as I go along. I do this to help grow myself. If I went on this journey to simply get recognition to keep me going, it would not always happen. I will not always have people recognize my work, but I must always set my mind to recognize the work I have done. To see the change through the challenge. If I did this to impress others, I would end up frustrated and lost. I would most likely give up more times than I would continue to press forward.

Keep creating future opportunities for yourself. Allow yourself to keep opening doors, not shutting them. Don't stop reaching. Don't allow the opinion of others to map out the future for you. To make a change in life, you might find yourself constantly shifting gears. As our circumstances change so will our viewpoint. Live each day feeling a sense of accomplishment in some area of your life and you will feel a greater motivation to push ahead.

> Live each day feeling a sense of accomplishment in some area of your life and you will feel a greater motivation to push ahead.

Live each day for the impact you can make, not chasing after the opportunities you feel you missed. The change will come in the way you approach each day. The impact will be in each interaction you make and in the way you challenge yourself. When we look towards the future there is much we can do. When we set our minds on making our lives impactful in some way, I believe that helps us to greater achievement of our goals. That is a driving force to motivate us to create and make a change. The change is ultimately for us, but we can influence others through the changes we make, thus making a change in not only ourselves, but possibly in the world around us as well. Think on that and focus on all you can do. Think of all the possibilities to make an impact. Think of all the opportunities that you can create.

There is no sense in living our lives going after missed opportunities. If we get into doing that, we will drain our energy, time, and focus. Missed opportunities are just that: missed. New possibilities are our future. Chasing after missed opportunities, if you really stop and think about it, sets us behind. Figure out what may have gone wrong and push ahead. There is a reason that something didn't work out as originally planned. It happens to all of us at some point in our lives in some way. However, don't focus for too long on that or you may lose your drive to move ahead. Each day we can make a change. Each day we can influence others. Each day we can grow ourselves. Live life seeking the best possibilities for yourself each day.

Think back to a time when you have tried something new. When you completed the task how did you feel? Did you feel good for having tried

The When

something different or accomplishing something you didn't think you would ever be able to do? Did you want to remember that moment? Now think back to a time when you motivated yourself to do a task. How did it make you feel when you were done?

All the time and effort you put towards your goal and the feeling created when you achieved it. Simply amazing right?!? Hold onto that feeling because there will be times in life where you will need to draw upon that experience.

Enjoy, that high you feel once you have accomplished what you set out to do and record it somewhere. We all experience the highs and lows of life. It is in the low moments that we will need to remember the high ones as we head on our journey. Change is difficult at times, but it can be really rewarding. When we believe in ourselves there is much we can achieve in life.

4 Ways to Make a Change

CHAPTER 6

You can!

I've chosen to title this chapter "You can" because simply put, you can. There is no one that truly stands in your way but you. You are able to do this. You are able to make the change. You are able to change your journey. You are able to create and take the steps to get there.

You might not be the best at everything, but it's about being the greatest you can be for you! It's the determination to make the change, especially when life hits you hard. Strive to do something better than you did the day before. Give yourself credit for trying, and choose to see the positive. Determine to make the change you want.

When life hits you hard, don't cave into feelings of doubt, fear, or inadequacy. You have a talent! We all do. Whether you are 2 or 102, we can all reach for more! Our goals will be different as we go through life, but our drive should always be there to make the change. We all have moments where life is rough. We must look to the reason we started during those times and push ahead. Slow down, take a breath, refocus and take in all you have done. Take in that moment. Keep striving: it is you, and you alone, for whom you are on this journey remember that!

My grandmother was in her 70s and went to college. She didn't get a degree, but she wanted to go to school and learn, so she did. That was a change in her life. People change careers, college majors, or goals in life every day. Change is all around us. How we embrace change in our life is up to us.

It is the constant determination in life that will help us through the difficulty and the challenges we face. We need to remember that we may not be the best at everything, and that is okay, because what we should be striving to do is be our best and see the constant change within ourselves. No two days will be exactly alike in our life, and if they were we might find it boring to be quite honest.

> There is something each day that you may have done that was better than the day before. The next day can be just as exciting also.

Seize every opportunity to celebrate the day. I think it is a great opportunity to be excited about what more you can do tomorrow. There is something each day that you may have done that was better than the day before. The next day can be just as exciting also. See yourself in a positive light every day. Stop challenging yourself to be any person other than, you. You have something to share. You have changes you want to make that are possible.

You can!

Life hits us all harder at different times. Focus on all your progress. Let it push you, motivate you, and challenge you in your journey through life.

One thing you should remember is to give yourself credit. Whether you are a full-time worker, parent, caregiver, student, or perhaps have a combination of these things and then some, we need to make sure we remind ourselves of that as we go through life. As you seek to make change, remember these other pieces also come in to play not just sometimes, but every day. It is no easy task to make a change as I mentioned before. The other elements are bound to add times of stress as well.

You must remind yourself that you are trying. There are days where you will need to remind yourself of that more than others. Always remember who you are. The fact that you are trying to balance all of those things in and of itself can be a lot. Add trying to change something else in your life and you might tend to feel even more overwhelmed. Look at all you have accomplished and know this also can be done. As I said earlier, if I never continued to reach for more, life would have been so different.

Making a change takes the ability for us to give ourselves credit where it is due. To give ourselves the recognition for trying to make a difference. If you are balancing it all, it's time you give yourself credit. Really focus on who you are as you work on what you want to change in your life. Remember: with each step you have done great things and are made to continue to do great things. There are only so many hours in a day and so many days in a week; we must use our time wisely so it doesn't escape us.

That includes celebrating our lives. We must celebrate the moments of accomplishment or change to help keep us focused on the many possibilities that are ahead. Celebration adds happiness to our life. Happiness helps our drive to move forward and embrace life to a greater degree. Keep climbing. Keep exploring. Keep celebrating.

That also includes doing more for ourselves. Think of it as painting the large canvas of your life one day at a time. Don't let another day simply pass you by. Don't just observe a landscape, create your own! Allow your passions and creativity to combine to create a nice picture. If you are working and do have all the other pieces in place, then keep at it and give yourself more credit. No one wins a race through simply getting up and running just one day. They train themselves each time they go out. They stretch to prepare for the race and then set up a plan or schedule to run a certain distance in preparation for the big race. Our mission to making a change and reaching our goals can be looked at in a similar way through preparation, time, and training. Preparation to come up with what the change is going to be, time in the way we look at setting up and managing our goals, and training in the way we reprogram our mindset and outlook and find ways to add in more celebration. You can do this!

Your journey will involve planning and preparation throughout, so give yourself time and credit. Sometimes we have too large an agenda for ourselves. We can achieve it all, but must work to absorb it in pieces. Think of a meeting you have attended with a full agenda. Did you feel more overwhelmed than having had absorbed the information? Probably so. Think of another meeting that was shorter and

> Your journey will involve planning and preparation throughout, so give yourself time and credit.

had only a couple of things to focus on. Did you take in more from that meeting? Probably. It's easier to absorb the information when given in smaller steps or broken down. Life can feel that way too at times. We must take time to break things down. We will learn more and achieve more if we do, and we owe that to ourselves.

Challenge yourself to take a step forward. Just one step. Record how you feel after taking that step. Mentally take it all in. Every emotion and feeling. Were you scared? Happy? Amazed at yourself for having tried? Then reward yourself for what you did. Did I say reward yourself for taking one step? Yes, I did. You earned a reward for having tried. There is no limit to celebrating your achievements. Whatever motivates you to keep moving forward and inspires you to believe in yourself, do it for you! Then keep trying to make another change until it becomes more and more natural for you to move forward. This is not easy, but then again neither is life.

Am I a motivational speaker? No. Do I do well with speaking in general? No. Do I wish I did? Yes. Do I wish I could speak to others and be a motivational speaker? Yes. However, my "What?" is to encourage other people. My "Why?" is because I have needed to do that very thing over and over again for myself. I am told I am encouraging, so I try to push myself to feed off of that. Find that special, unique quality about yourself also. How I do this will continually change, but one way I strive to make a change is by pushing myself forward in this area. I teach seminars at work to grow myself or talk to people about starting a business, etc. These are small steps on my way to growth and change in my life.

I'm not afraid of public speaking. I don't necessarily consider myself a natural at it either. So, I try to balance by taking small strides in doing new things. I believe at times I am being my own worst critic as well. I think we all have a tendency to do this to ourselves. I fight this through looking at various obstacles I have overcome and I try to move ahead a little more through volunteering for projects or things that might be new or difficult. You know what? With each opportunity I take on I grow. I change. I overcome.

At times I feel I struggle with social anxiety, so some situations might be more of a struggle than others, but I push to not let it get the best of me! I think we all may struggle socially in different areas or with certain situations at times if we are honest. I know I need to push back thoughts of comparison or wanting recognition in order to feel accepted harder to make them take a back seat in my life. There is much I can do and there is much you can do also. Change is what it is: change. Embrace it and don't lose yourself in the process. Think of change in life like you would learning something new. You don't instantly know it, you learn through training. Training is done in steps and stages. The same can also be said about change in life. It is through steps and stages and trial and error that we train ourselves in living a new way of life.

If I don't try, I'll never know. This is one of many reasons to continue to try in life. Could I be a speaker? Of course, but I must work at it in different ways to make it become a reality for me. If I simply wish it into existence, I will be setting myself up for disappointment. I must work towards it to create the change that is possible. Wishing and doing are two

You can!

different things. I can wish all I want, but if I am not willing to move, my wish will just be that. I strive each day to create different possibilities for myself. If I can encourage people along the way, what a great impact I have made. Each day I think of new ways that I can grow in different areas of my life. Some days I may move farther ahead than others, but I always strive to simply move forward.

If I didn't, I would not be where I am today. I don't say it to be prideful. I say it to be real. This is hard stuff. I do know that all it takes is believing in you. Always wanting, but fearful to change is sometimes a part of all of us, but we must dig, push and strive to gain the strength to move ahead. Am I going to reach out and try in life? Yes. On the days I just don't feel it, I dig deep and push harder. Do I have those days? Yes. A lot of them. Is it tough? It's really tough, but you have to. You have to try. You have to do it for you because no one else will. You have to reach when you don't want to. To stretch and to try when no one else is cheering you on.

The key is also learning to laugh at yourself in life. Don't take change so seriously that you forget laughter in your life. Let me tell you, I add a whole lot of laughter in my life. I like to share my funny stories with others also. I once glued a 500-piece puzzle to the floor trying to preserve it for my kids. Yep! I glued one side and thought it was dry only to flip it over and spray the other side and find out a day later it was glued to my kitchen floor! I learned that day to find an easier way to preserve the puzzle next time and not to use glue on a puzzle on the floor. Remember, I said always keep learning in life. I have a bunch of stories I can share, and perhaps will have the opportunity in the future through my writing, but make sure to laugh in life. Get comfortable laughing at yourself. That is key to growth as well.

I think we all can say we have crazy moments in our lives. We simply need to learn different ways to navigate through them. Always strive to learn and grow throughout your life. Look at all of your experiences as well. Always seek to continue to laugh, learn and grow in life.

You have to move forward, and the key is one step at a time. Make today the day you map out the future of change for yourself one step at a time. There are four ways to make a change, and those four involve tough questions that will both pull you out of your comfort zone and reward you. Ask yourself "What?", "Why?", "How?", and "When?" Let the answers to those questions help shape the goals you set and changes you want to make. Learn to reach for more and reach beyond yourself. Sometimes taking a step in a new direction isn't missed opportunities, but simply new possibilities. Sometimes it is one more step in learning how to *DO-4-U*!

> Sometimes taking a step in a new direction isn't missed opportunities, but simply new possibilities.

ABOUT THE AUTHOR

Kristina Gipe received her Bachelor's Degree in Business, Management, and Economics with a concentration in Business Administration from Empire State College. The Lord placed it on her heart to write her first book 15 Days of Love, where she began her journey and found an undiscovered passion for writing. Kristina continues to write to encourage others.

www.do-4-u.com

OTHER BOOKS BY KRISTINA GIPE:

- 15 Days Of Love
- Cast Your Cares
- Happy In Hope

Made in the USA
Monee, IL
23 July 2021